# Me And MYCAT

## STEPHEN BAKER
### AUTHOR OF *HOW TO LIVE WITH A NEUROTIC CAT*

*Illustrated By Gerry Gersten*

**WARNER BOOKS**

A Time Warner Company

*Because there's only one cat*
*like your cat*

Copyright © 1992 by Stephen Baker Associates, Inc.
All rights reserved.

Warner Books, Inc., 1271 Avenue of the Americas, New York, NY 10020

 A Time Warner Company

Printed in the United States of America
First Printing: December 1992
10  9  8  7  6  5  4  3  2  1

**ISBN: 0-446-39455-6**

*Cover design by Carmine Vecchio*

*Cover illustration by Gerry Gersten*

# Contents

# Introduction

ME & MY CAT is about *you* and *your* cat. Here's a chance to follow your favorite four-legged friend from kittenhood to adulthood, step by step, mischief by mischief.

YOU are the author of this book—a permanent record of your life with your cat. Simply fill in the blanks, and put it all between covers. This can be your and your cat's photo album, too—special pages are provided for snapshots. And there is space for miscellaneous memorabilia: pedigrees, awards, medical history, travel, high spots, dates and places you want to remember ever and again.

So grab your pencil or pen, your camera, or anything that leaves a mark on paper. The day may not far away when you will want to share your thoughts and observations with friends and relatives, cat lovers and cat haters—and maybe *even* your cat.

A word of caution, however. Do not *ever* let your cat see this album. It may not agree with what you have to say, tear up and eat the pages of ME & MY CAT purely out of spite.

Stephen Baker

P.S. If you have more than one cat, you may want to have another diary for your other cat(s).

**THIS BOOK IS ABOUT**

_____

(CAT'S NAME)

**WITH LOVE FROM**



_____

# My cat is

| | | | |
|---|---|---|---|
| Abyssinian | ___ | British/European Shorthair | ___ |
| Angora | ___ | American/Domestic | |
| Calico | ___ | Shorthair | ___ |
| Chinese | ___ | Tabby | ___ |
| Natasha | ___ | Tortoise Shell | ___ |
| Pampas | ___ | Turkish Angora | ___ |
| Seal Point | ___ | Manx (short-haired) | ___ |
| Spanish | ___ | Russian Blue | ___ |
| Domestic Shorthair | ___ | Turkish Van | ___ |
| Archangel | ___ | Ragdoll | ___ |
| Short-haired Persian | ___ | Japanese Bobtail | ___ |
| American Wirehair | ___ | Korat | ___ |
| Scottish Fold | ___ | Peke-faced Persian | ___ |
| Egyptian Mau | ___ | Burmese | ___ |
| Cheshire | ___ | Cornish Rex | ___ |
| Ocicat | ___ | Devon Rex | ___ |
| Burmese/Malayan | ___ | Siamese | ___ |
| Somali (long-haired | | Colorpoint Shorthair | |
| Abyssinian) | ___ | (Siamese with tabby, | |
| Norwegian Forest Cat | ___ | tortie, or red point | |
| Persian Van | ___ | colors) | ___ |
| Persian | ___ | Tonkinese | ___ |
| Himalayan | ___ | Oriental/Foreign Shorthair | ___ |
| Geoffroy | ___ | Brown Havana | ___ |
| Cymric (long-haired Manx) | ___ | Bombay | ___ |
| Margay | ___ | _____ | |
| Chartreux | ___ | _____ | |
| Pallas | ___ | _____ | |
| Maine Coon | ___ | All (or some) of the above | ___ |
| Balinese/Javanese | ___ | | |

# My cat's name is

— — — — — — — — — — — — — — — —

Why the name?

_____

_____

_____

_____

_____

Other names
considered

_____

_____

THAT'S WHAT MY
OWNER CALLS ME.
DON'T ASK WHAT
I CALL MY OWNER.

BIRTHPLACE

BIRTHDATE

# The Beginning

All cats start out by being born—as auspicious a beginning
as one can expect. Cannily, they start out as "cuddly little kittens."
Jot down all that comes to mind about your cat's kittenhood.
What were your first impressions? What do you think
your cat's first impressions were?

When was your cat born (day, hour)? _____

_____

Where was your cat born (indoors? outdoors? at someone else's

home? which room?) _____

_____

_____

What made you decide to pick your cat over the others? _____

_____

How long did your cat stay with its family? _____

Were there any surprises? _____

_____

_____

Other comments _____

_____

_____

## GREAT MOMENTS, GREAT MILESTONES

| ACTIVITY | WHEN |
| --- | --- |
| **Kitten opens its eyes** | |
| **Kitten starts crawling** | |
| **Kitten meows** | |
| **Kitten discovers rest of house** | |
| **Kitten goes outdoors** | |
| **Kitten feeds from its bowl** | |
| **Kitten uses litterbox** | |
| **Kitten is weaned from its mother** | |
| **Kitten responds to its name** | |

# I was adopted!

Not all cats are to the manner born. Has yours popped into your living room quite unexpectedly—like a visitor from who knows where? Do you recall your first encounter with your cat? What was it that made you want to adopt your cat? Have you ever regretted having been so soft of heart? Who adopted whom anyway?

The first few weeks _____

_____

_____

_____

_____

_____

FORMER OWNER

- - - - - - - - - -

PRESENT OWNER

- - - - - - - - - -

DATE OF ARRIVAL

- - - - - - - - - -

# At home at last!
## (FAMOUS FIRSTS)

First meal _____

_____

First night _____

_____

First discovery _____

_____

First toy, first game _____

_____

_____

First trip (near or far) _____

_____

_____

First mischief _____

_____

Other firsts _____

_____

_____

_____

# My cat—hello everybody!

# The Family
## (As far as you can tell . . .)

Mother (color, breed, etc.) _____

_____

_____

Father _____

_____

_____

And the others _____

_____

## GREAT
## GRANDPARENTS

N  _____
BD _____
BP _____
C  _____
B  _____

N  _____
BD _____
BP _____
C  _____
B  _____

N  _____
BD _____
BP _____
C  _____
B  _____

N  _____
BD _____
BP _____
C  _____
B  _____

N  _____
BD _____
BP _____
C  _____
B  _____

N  _____
BD _____
BP _____
C  _____
B  _____

N  _____
BD _____
BP _____
C  _____
B  _____

N  _____
BD _____
BP _____
C  _____
B  _____

## GRANDPARENTS

N  _____
BD _____
BP _____
C  _____
B  _____

N  _____
BD _____
BP _____
C  _____
B  _____

N  _____
BD _____
BP _____
C  _____
B  _____

N  _____
BD _____
BP _____
C  _____
B  _____

## PARENTS

N  _____
BD _____
BP _____
C  _____
B  _____

N  _____
BD _____
BP _____
C  _____
B  _____

## HERE I AM!

N  _____
BD _____
BP _____
C  _____
B  _____

N    Name
BD   Birthday
BP   Birthplace
C    Color
B    Breed (if any)

15

# Mommy Who?

For several months, the most important person (after you, of course) in your cat's life will be its mother. Tell us about the happy family. Is mother cat taking good care of her kittens? How often has she given birth before? Has she ever had the same mate more than once to start a family? Or is she the type who prefers variety? With whom? Whose ideas was it to have babies anyway? His? Hers? Yours?

_____

_____

_____

_____

_____

_____

_____

**SIZE OF LITTER(S)**

**When**

First _____  _____

Second _____  _____

Third _____  _____

Fourth _____  _____

Others _____  _____

_____  _____

_____  _____

I DO!

# Daddy $\left(\genfrac{}{}{0pt}{}{\text{CAT}}{\genfrac{}{}{0pt}{}{\text{ABOUT}}{\text{TOWN}}}\right)$ Who?

Most male cats fancy themselves as God's gift to the opposite sex. Their approach is less than subtle. Macho to the core, they believe in one-night stands, love 'em and leave 'em. Describe the father—as much as you had a chance to find out. How did he and your cat's mother meet? Has he been heard from since? Where is he now? (If you don't know, you're not alone. Don't even bother calling the Missing Persons Bureau.)

He is (description) _____

_____

_____

_____

I DON'T!

He also had a crush on: (other objects of his affection) _____

_____

_____

_____

I don't know what she saw in him. He was a

|  | Yes | No | Probably |
|---|---|---|---|
| Bum |  |  |  |
| Liar |  |  |  |
| Sneak |  |  |  |
| Boor |  |  |  |
| Lecher |  |  |  |
| Cheat |  |  |  |
| All of the above |  |  |  |

# Brothers & Sisters Who?

Does your cat have brothers and sisters? Kittens rarely enter
this world alone. Any signs of sibling rivalry? Which parent
have the kittens taken after?

Brothers _____

_____

_____

Sisters _____

_____

_____

Family resemblances (in looks and attitude) _____

_____

_____

Family differences (in looks and attitude) _____

_____

_____

Comments _____

_____

_____

**THE FAMILY THAT STAYS TOGETHER TAKES UP A LOT OF SPACE.**

# My cat's official
# Pawprints

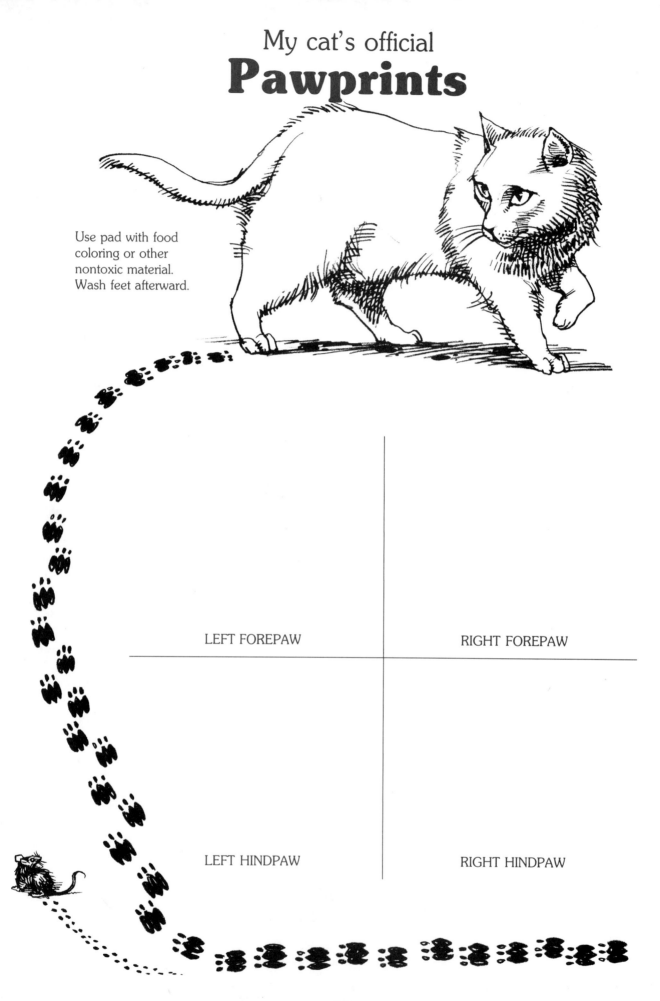

Use pad with food coloring or other nontoxic material. Wash feet afterward.

LEFT FOREPAW

RIGHT FOREPAW

LEFT HINDPAW

RIGHT HINDPAW

# Vital (and not so vital) statistics

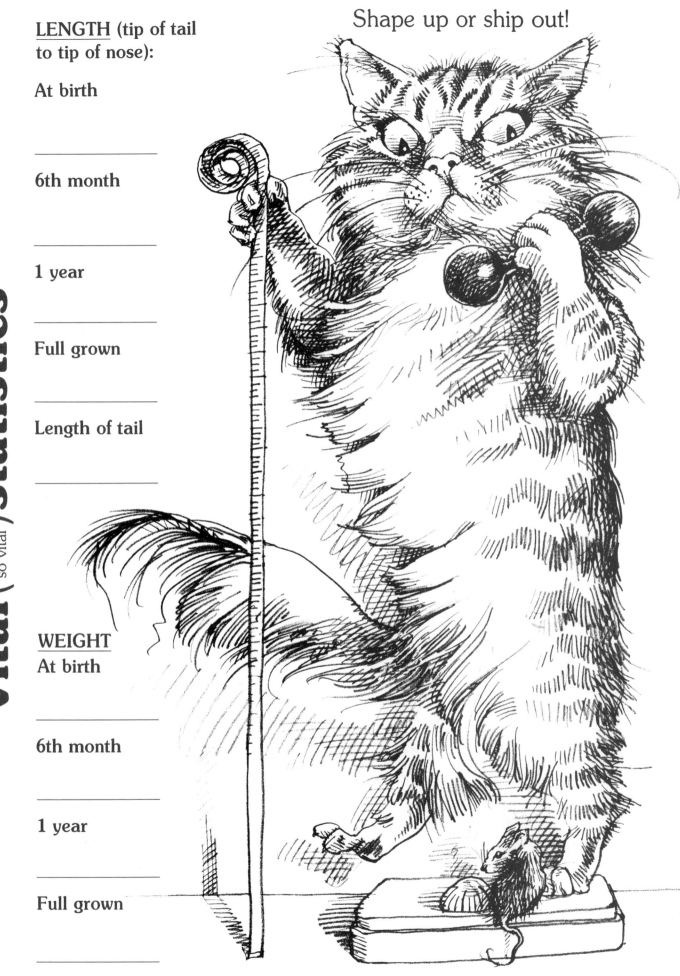

**LENGTH** (tip of tail to tip of nose):

At birth

_____

6th month

_____

1 year

_____

Full grown

_____

Length of tail

_____

**WEIGHT**
At birth

_____

6th month

_____

1 year

_____

Full grown

_____

Shape up or ship out!

21

# Color me gorgeous!

Fill in your cat's color. Use pencil, paint, ink, crayon, felt pen, or whatever you can find. If you don't have the exact color, try getting close.

MY EYES ARE ———————

COLOR ME DISH

My cat's color is (check off more than one if need be, as in calico, tabby, piebald, etc.):

|  | YES | NO | COULD BE |
|---|---|---|---|
| BLACK | ☐ | ☐ | ☐ |
| BLUE | ☐ | ☐ | ☐ |
| CHESTNUT | ☐ | ☐ | ☐ |
| LAVENDER | ☐ | ☐ | ☐ |
| PIEBALD | ☐ | ☐ | ☐ |
| RED | ☐ | ☐ | ☐ |
| CREAM | ☐ | ☐ | ☐ |
| SILVER | ☐ | ☐ | ☐ |
| ORANGE | ☐ | ☐ | ☐ |
| TABBY | ☐ | ☐ | ☐ |
| GRAY | ☐ | ☐ | ☐ |
| BLOND | ☐ | ☐ | ☐ |
| SNOW WHITE | ☐ | ☐ | ☐ |
| OFF WHITE | ☐ | ☐ | ☐ |
| PINK | ☐ | ☐ | ☐ |
| CARROT | ☐ | ☐ | ☐ |
| TAN | ☐ | ☐ | ☐ |
| REDDISH-BROWN | ☐ | ☐ | ☐ |

OTHER

———————————————————

———————————————————

MY CAT'S COLOR DEFIES DESCRIPTION ———————

# Here's looking at you

**Everything you always wanted to know about photographing your cat:**
All you need is a camera, film, and (it helps!) the cat. If your subject is in the mood for having its picture taken, bless your stars. Unless there are dribbles of Cheshire in your cat's blood, forget about the "smile, you're on camera" opening gambit.

The secret of good composition lies in simplicity. Resist the temptation to include everything. Usually, the nearer, the better the picture. Unless, it's the landscape you want.

Know your equipment. It is difficult to take sharp, well-defined images of cats flying through space, or sitting in a dark corner unless you use flash light and have the reflexes of a quarterback playing at the Superbowl. Your odds for a clearer picture will noticeably improve outdoors, especially on a sunny day. Special close-up lenses (widely available) make extreme close-ups possible—closer than three feet. The smaller the aperture, the sharper the picture, provided you have the light. It pays to talk to the experts—experts on photography first, cats second.

# Draw me!

Cats are not as difficult to put on paper (and we don't mean litter box) as it seems. Give it a try. You may surprise yourself and your cat.

**Start with a circle.**
(Use a compass if you have one.) Add ears, eyes, whiskers, spots and color, in that order. Follow the same approach (outline first, details second) in drawing the body. If your cat won't sit still (i.e., if it isn't fast asleep), use photos for reference.

# Wax poetic

Cats inspire words—both epithets and eulogies. Here's your chance to put it on paper. A verse maybe?

_____

_____

_____

_____

_____

_____

*Here's a sample—with
apologies to Carl Sandburg*

*"The cat comes
  on little fog feet
  he jumps onto my lap
  'cause that's his seat."*

———————————————

_____   _____

_____   _____

_____   _____

_____   _____

29

Still more poems _____

_____

_____

_____

_____

_____

_____

_____

_____

_____

_____

_____

_____

_____

_____

(paste in
photograph
of your cat
sitting on top
of pedestal)

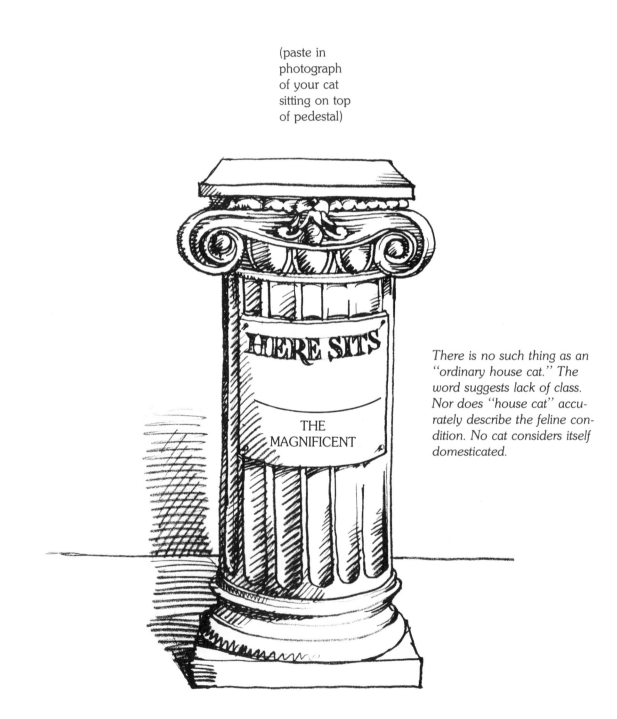

HERE SITS

THE
MAGNIFICENT

*There is no such thing as an "ordinary house cat." The word suggests lack of class. Nor does "house cat" accurately describe the feline condition. No cat considers itself domesticated.*

# Not just any cat . . .

Paste in a copy of
pedigree certificate or any
other registration form
that you may have. (If
you have none, use page
for photographs. Your cat
is special just the same—
hey, it's your cat, isn't it?)

**My cat talks! First**

**(second, third, fourth) words**

# I talk to my cat: My first

A cat can get the best—and the worst—of you. Have you ever told your cat what was on your mind? If you did, join the club.

| Terms of endearment | Terms of estrangement |
| --- | --- |
| _____ | _____ |
| _____ | _____ |
| _____ | _____ |
| _____ | _____ |
| _____ | _____ |
| _____ | _____ |
| _____ | _____ |
| _____ | _____ |

# second, third, etc.) words

# Gifts, gifts, gifts

"If you love me as much as you say, show me," your cat purrs. What have you brought your four-legged friend as of late—if anything? Here's your chance to make a list of all the goodies and settle the matter once and for all.

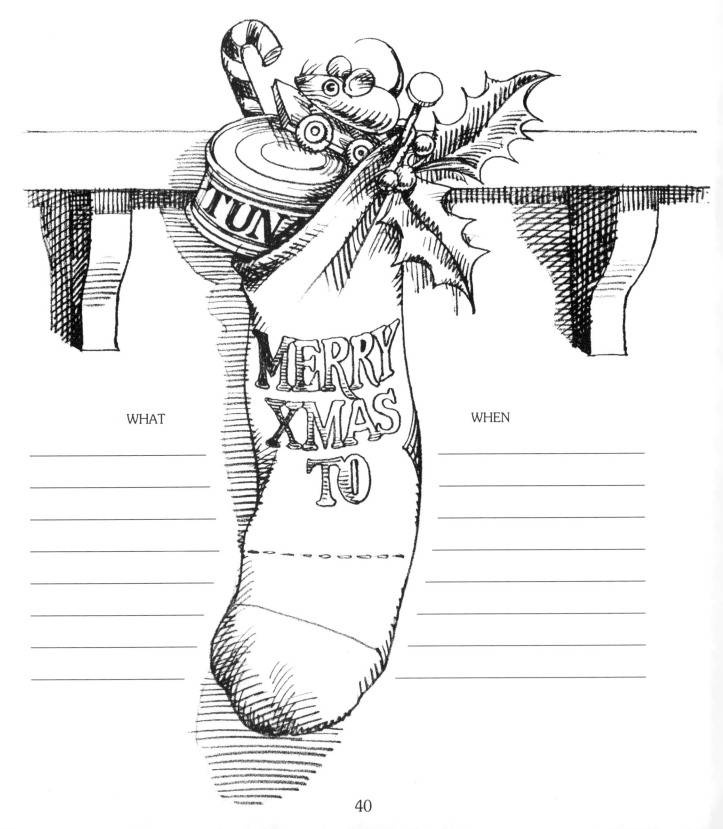

WHAT

WHEN

# My cat plays

# and plays . . .

# and plays

## Favorite games, favorite toys

"All work and no play" is "all play and no work" to any cat worth its whiskers. What about your cat?

_____

_____

_____

_____

_____

_____

_____

_____

_____

_____

_____

# Favorite games, favorite toys (cont.)

45

_____    _____

_____    _____

_____    _____

_____    _____

_____    _____

_____    _____

_____    _____

_____    _____

_____    _____

_____    _____

THE FLYING
MACHINE

NAPOLEON

SUPERCAT

# My cat thinks it is . . .

Cats have vivid imaginations. Take a picture of your cat's face (in color or black and white), blow it up to size (photographically or xerographically), then cut silhouette of print with scissors or single-edged razorblade to paste it over the face of whoever comes closest to your cat's alter ego. Use rubber cement or any common paper glue. If any part of drawing shows from behind photo, use white correction fluid or paint to cover it.

BEAUTY QUEEN                    KING OF THE BEASTS

49

STONEFACE

JUMPING JACK

A BIRD!

MASTER OF THE UNIVERSE

RIP VAN WINKLE

# Who else?

_____

_____

_____

_____

_____

_____

_____

# Me and my cat

To your cat you <u>are</u> someone special. Without you there would be no food on the table, no bed to sleep on, no television to watch. How does your cat show its affection for you? Licking your face? Swishing its tail, pricking up its ears? Purring? Meowing, hissing? Blinking, staring? Cuddling up?

General comments _____

_____

_____

_____

_____

When happy _____

_____

_____

When unhappy _____

_____

_____

_____

When hungry _____

_____

_____

_____

_____

_____

_____

When it wants your attention _____

_____

_____

When just as soon not have your attention _____

_____

_____

_____

_____

_____

With love

_____

(YOUR NAME GOES HERE)

# Us and my cat

How do your friends, relatives, members of your family, feel about <u>your</u> cat? Sign them off on the dotted lines.

_____

_____

_____

_____

_____

_____

Blow up of photo of people
and cat goes inside heart.
Cut in shape of heart
and paste in position.

*Everybody sign up!*

---

# Us and my cat (cont.)

# My cat thinks it is a dog

Casting a jaundiced eye on their canine roommates, cats are often under the impression they are but a new—and vastly improved—breed of dog. Never mind if they can't wag their tails as expertly or if their meow is a far cry from bow-wow. Look at it this way: Their purr does sound like a growl, right? And they can jump in your lap as well as—or better than—any dog. What's your own shaggy dog-cat story?

Has your cat convinced you yet that really it's a dog in cat's clothing?

_____

_____

_____

_____

_____

_____

How does the "other" dog (the true version) feel about your cat trying to fake it?

_____

_____

_____

_____

# My cat thinks it is my baby

I am

_____
BABY'S NAME

Competing with a human infant can be a trying experience for a cat. A baby is a larger animal; it has a louder voice; from your cat's point of view it lacks both intellect and coordination yet has a way of gaining more attention. How does your cat react to this latest addition to the family?

_____

_____

_____

_____

_____

_____

_____

_____

_____

| BABY'S NAME | BABY'S DATE OF BIRTH |
|---|---|
|  |  |
|  |  |

# Best friends

Your cat probably has its own circle of friends. They could be a human being, another pet, any creature of the wild.

Who are they? What experiences do they share? _____

_____

_____

_____

_____

_____

Yours
Truly

# More best friends

# Best friends (cont.)

# When you have more than one

There may be other cats in your home. Who are they? How are they different? What are their personalities?

_____

_____

_____

_____

_____

_____

Yours Truly
—again

A touch of jealousy perhaps? _____

_____

Any fights lately? Domestic squabbles? _____

_____

_____

_____

_____

Oh, they get along just fine (well, most of the time) _____  __


_____

_____

_____

_____

_____

_____

_____

_____

_____

_____

_____

_____

My cat is intrigued by the sight of

**Chicken** ☐

**Blackbird** ☐

**Finch** ☐

**Canary** ☐

**Sparrow** ☐

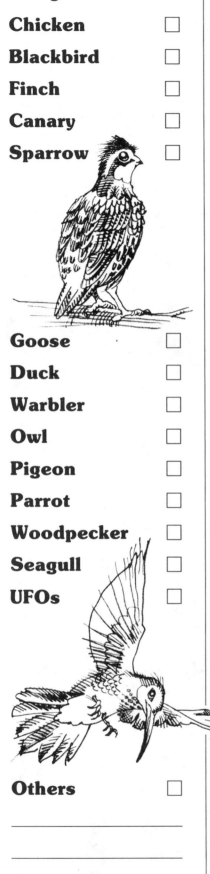

**Goose** ☐

**Duck** ☐

**Warbler** ☐

**Owl** ☐

**Pigeon** ☐

**Parrot** ☐

**Woodpecker** ☐

**Seagull** ☐

**UFOs** ☐

**Others** ☐

_____

_____

_____

# My cat . . .
# The Birdwatcher

For reasons best known to themselves, cats seem to enjoy watching anthing that moves up and down, or even sideways—probably in the hope of putting a stop to all the activity with one decisive swoop of the paw.

_____

_____

_____

_____

_____

_____

_____

_____

_____

_____

_____

_____

# My cat . . .
# The Hunter

Remembering the good old days, some cats still fancy themselves as hunters *extraordinaire*.

_____

_____

_____

_____

Name some of your cat's favorite small game—or big game, for that matter.

**Mice** ☐
**Roaches** ☐
**Goldfish** ☐
**Lizards** ☐
**Frogs** ☐
**Butterflies** ☐
**Crickets** ☐
**Small dogs** ☐
**Big dogs** ☐

**Pillows** ☐
**Soap bubbles** ☐
**Crocheted balls** ☐
**Lampshades** ☐

**Others** ☐

_____

_____

_____

_____

_____

BEWARE!

More about my cat, the predator _____

_____

_____

_____

_____

_____

_____

_____

Surprise! Look what my cat brought home. _____

_____

_____

_____

_____

_____

_____

# Stalking, tracking, chasing,

# pouncing, prowling, leaping . . .

# doing what comes naturally

# My cat grooms

Cleanliness is next to catliness.

# Scratch me, please

Cats welcome being scratched any time, any place; lying down, sitting, standing, walking, hanging from the chandelier. How about your cat's "scratch me, please" wills and pleasure? What are his spots of choice? Ears, forehead, nose, neck, shoulders, back, forepaw, hindpaw, belly, rump? Show order of preference—the cat's, not yours.

1 _ _ _ _ _ _ _ _ _ _ _

2 _ _ _ _ _ _ _ _ _ _

3 _ _ _ _ _ _ _ _ _ _

4 _ _ _ _ _ _ _ _ _ _

5 _ _ _ _ _ _ _ _ _ _

6 _ _ _ _ _ _ _ _ _ _ _

Do you and your cat have yet to come to an understanding as to a mutually satisfactory scratching routine? _ _ _ _ _ _ _ _ _ _ _

_ _ _ _ _ _ _ _ _ _ _ _ _ _ _ _ _ _ _ _ _ _ _ _ _

**Scratch my back and I'll scratch yours.**

# My cat goes up . . .

What goes up must come down!

My cat comes down

# My cat is crazy

Normal cats do not act normally. That would be most uncatlike.
Having lived with your cat long enough, do you agree? Yes?

Yes! Proof No. 1 _____

_____

_____

Yes! Proof No. 2 _____

_____

_____

Yes! Proof No. 3 _____

_____

_____

_____

_____

Yes! Proof No. 4 _____

_____

_____

Yes! Proof No. 5 _____

_____

_____

_____

_____

_____

Yes! Proof No. 6 _____

_____

_____

Be your cat's own psychologist.
Would you say your cat is an
☐ introvert
☐ extrovert
☐ ambivert?
Or just a plain nut _____

Explain _____

_____

_____

_____

_____

Does your cat . . .

# Feline Normalcy Test (FNT)*

|  | YES | NO |
|---|---|---|
| Swat at nonexistent flies? | ☐ | ☐ |
| Run across the room exceeding legal speed limit? | ☐ | ☐ |
| Insist upon being the centerpiece on your dinner table? | ☐ | ☐ |
| Lie across pages of newspaper covering the story you want to read? | ☐ | ☐ |
| Sub for a bookend on your bookshelf? | ☐ | ☐ |
| Enjoy singing—with or without you? | ☐ | ☐ |
| Climb the curtains? | ☐ | ☐ |
| Appropriate your entire bed pillow? | ☐ | ☐ |
| Consider your leg the best scratching post available? | ☐ | ☐ |
| Disagree with your choice of television programs? | ☐ | ☐ |
| Sit right in front of you on the dashboard while you're driving? | ☐ | ☐ |
| Consider the kitchen sink her bed of choice after mealtime? | ☐ | ☐ |
| Think of your closet as a private chamber built exclusively for cats? | ☐ | ☐ |
| Have a place at the dining table? | ☐ | ☐ |
| Take up more space on your bed than you do? | ☐ | ☐ |

*"Yes" answers show your cat is perfectly normal.

# My cat is crazy

# My cat is crazy. More proof.

# My cat eats

It is not true that cats sleep <u>all</u> day long. They take time out to eat. Some pick at their food. Others swallow food whole to save time. What are your cat's feeding habits?

Eating schedule: _____

_____

_____

**Where's the beef?**

Does your cat ever join you at the table? _____

_____

_____

# Food my cat likes

_____

_____

_____

_____

_____

_____

_____

_____

_____

_____

_____

_____

_____

_____

# Food my cat hates

_____

_____

_____

_____

_____

_____

_____

_____

_____

_____

_____

_____

_____

_____

Cats come from a carnivorous ancestry but that was some time ago. Today's cat is truly omnivorous and will eat anything edible—or inedible. What are some of the goodies that make your cat's whiskers quiver with anticipation?

CAT FOOD ☐

DOG FOOD ☐

YOUR FOOD ☐

RASPBERRY ICE CREAM ☐

BLOODY MARY ☐

WATERMELON ☐

GREEN OLIVES ☐

CAVIAR (BLACK) ☐

JELLY BEANS ☐

PEANUT BUTTER SANDWICH ☐

CHOCOLATE COOKIES ☐

POMPANO WITH ALMONDS ☐

MILK SHAKE ☐

VEAL CORDON BLEU ☐

LIVE COCKROACHES ☐

FISH TERIYAKI (BROILED) ☐

RIS DE VEAU MEUNIÈRE ☐

MOUSSE AU CHOCOLAT ☐

ANTIPASTO ☐

CABERNET SAUVIGNON (1979) ☐

GOLDFISH ☐

CHRISTMAS TREE
 DECORATIONS ☐

CHEWING GUM ☐

CANARY ☐

THIS WEEK'S _TV GUIDE_ ☐

HOUSEPLANTS ☐

EAU DE TOILETTE SPRAY ☐

ROLL OF BATHROOM TISSUE ☐

# My cat sleeps

My cat sleeps

Cats need plenty of rest; theirs is a full schedule, what with walking to and from the kitchen, keeping a close watch on the birds outside the window, jumping on and off your bed several times a day. What are your cat's sleeping habits?

My cat's sleeping schedule _____

_____

_____

**FAVORITE RESTING PLACES**

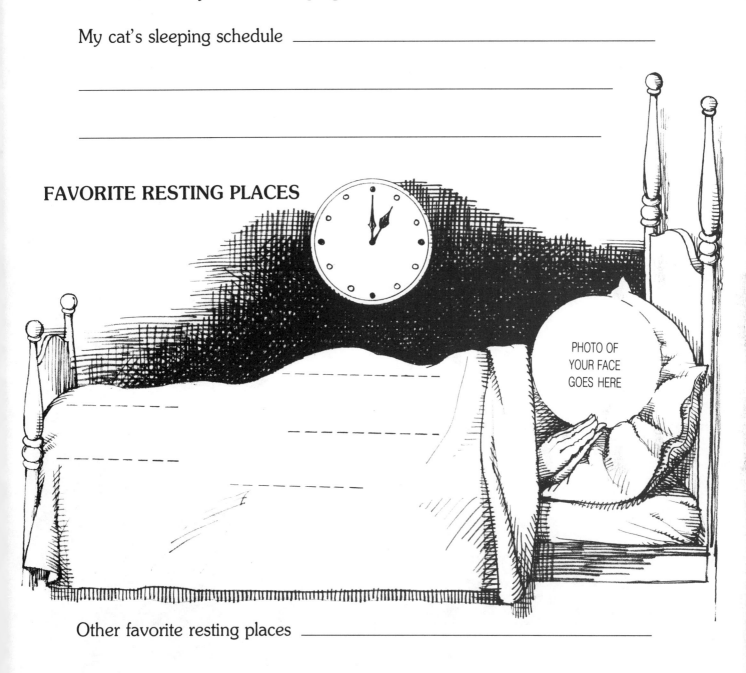

PHOTO OF
YOUR FACE
GOES HERE

Other favorite resting places _____

_____

_____

_____

_____

# It's 12 P.M. . . . . Do you know where your cat is?

# Let me guess

# Have cat, will travel

Cats make good traveling companions—in their opinion, at least. Do you agree? Or don't you?

My favorite travel stories _____

**Don't leave home without me!**

_____

_____

_____

_____

_____

_____

_____

_____

_____

_____

_____

_____

_____

_____

_____

_____

_____

_____

## AND MY CAT WAS THERE, TOO

When                                    Where

_____         _____

_____         _____

_____         _____

_____         _____

_____         _____

_____         _____

_____         _____

# My cat, the traveler

# My cat, the student

You might have tried teaching your cat a trick or two. Keep trying. Sooner or later, it will catch on. A lifetime just may do it. What has ever reached your cat's ears?

My cat knows (I think) _____

_____

_____

_____

_____

| Lesson | Results (if any) |
|--------|------------------|
| _____ | _____ |
| _____ | _____ |
| _____ | _____ |
| _____ | _____ |

Lesson Results (if any)

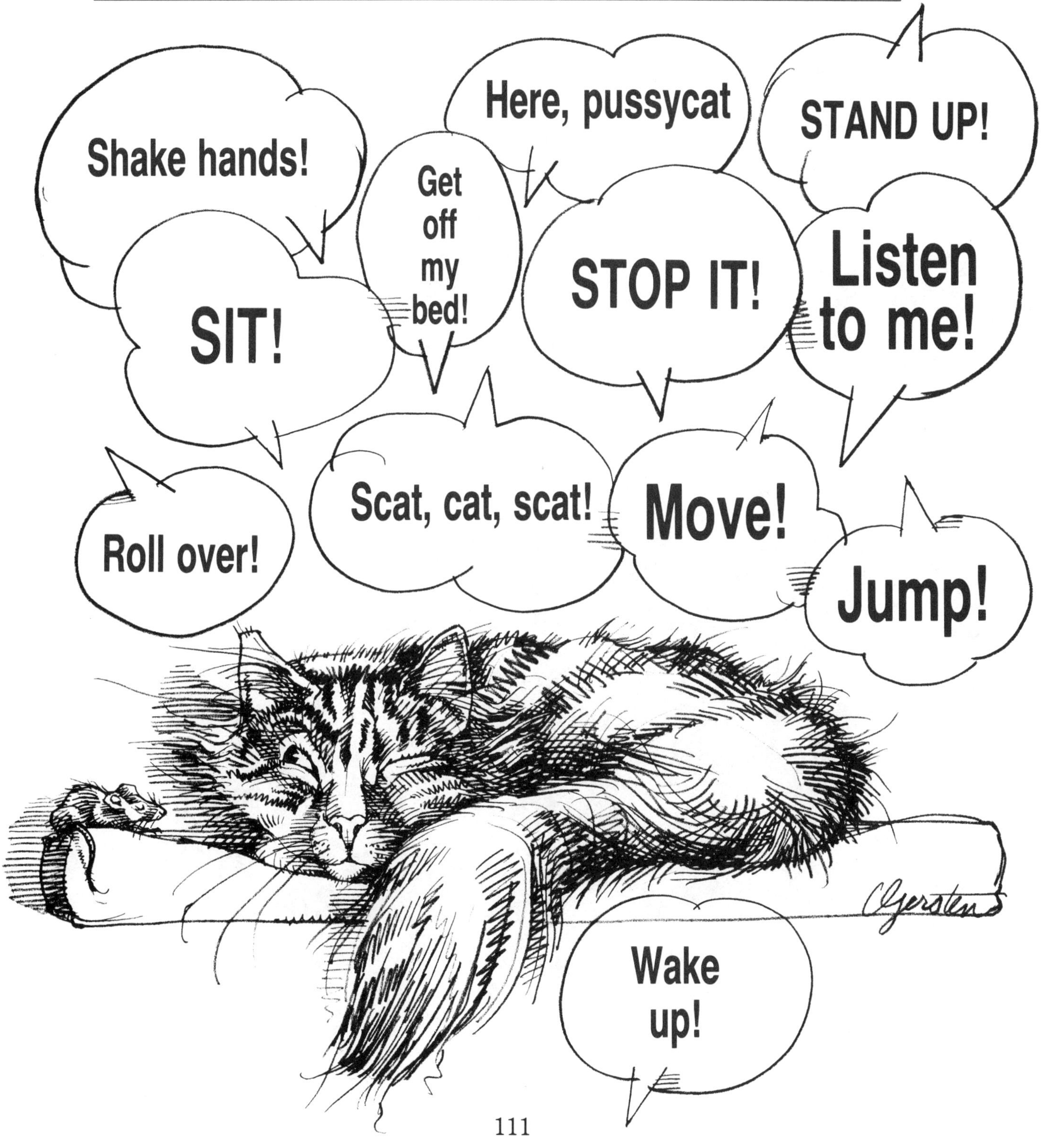

If your cat is as beautiful as everybody (including the cat) thinks it is, then it's for all the world to see it . . . If you have ever taken your cat to a show, here's your chance to tell about it.

Getting ready—me and my cat _____

_____

_____

_____

_____

Getting there is half the fun (or is it?) _____

_____

_____

_____

We're ready! _____

_____

_____

**The Show-off** (YOU OR YOUR CAT)

Coat _____

_____

_____

Head _____

_____

_____

_____

_____

Body _____

_____

_____

_____

_____

_____

Eyes _____

_____

_____

Color _____

_____

_____

_____

Other points (balance, refinement, etc.) _____

_____

_____

_____

115

# WE WENT, WE SAW, WE CONQUERED

| When | Where | Awards, certificates, mentions, decorations |
| --- | --- | --- |
| | | |
| | | |
| | | |
| | | |
| | | |
| | | |
| | | |
| | | |
| | | |
| | | |
| | | |
| | | |
| | | |
| | | |
| | | |
| | | |
| | | |
| | | |
| | | |
| | | |

| When | Where | Awards, certificates, mentions, decorations |
|------|-------|---------------------------------------------|
| _____ | _____ | _____ |
| _____ | _____ | _____ |
| _____ | _____ | _____ |
| _____ | _____ | _____ |
| _____ | _____ | _____ |
| _____ | _____ | _____ |
| _____ | _____ | _____ |
| _____ | _____ | _____ |
| _____ | _____ | _____ |
| _____ | _____ | _____ |
| _____ | _____ | _____ |
| _____ | _____ | _____ |
| _____ | _____ | _____ |
| _____ | _____ | _____ |
| _____ | _____ | _____ |
| _____ | _____ | _____ |
| _____ | _____ | _____ |

Judges' comments (overall assessment and condition) _____

_____

_____

_____

_____

# My Cat, the Beautiful

# My cat and the vet

## HEALTH RECORD

| Vaccinations | Date and Vet Visited | Date of Booster Shots |
|---|---|---|
| | | |
| | | |
| | | |
| | | |
| | | |
| | | |
| | | |

| Tests | Date and Vet Visited | Date of Follow-up Visits |
|---|---|---|
| | | |
| | | |
| | | |
| | | |
| | | |
| | | |
| | | |

| Illnesses | Date and Vet Visited | Medication | Home Treatment |
|---|---|---|---|
|  |  |  |  |
|  |  |  |  |
|  |  |  |  |
|  |  |  |  |
|  |  |  |  |
|  |  |  |  |
|  |  |  |  |
|  |  |  |  |
|  |  |  |  |
|  |  |  |  |
|  |  |  |  |

## My (if not my cat's) favorite vet

Name _____     Name _____

Address _____     Address _____

Phone _____     Phone _____

Name _____     Name _____

Address _____     Address _____

Phone _____     Phone _____


Hospitals _____


Pet insurance _____

# Who's who in my cat's life

## Cat Sitters (neighbors, relatives, friends, etc.)

Name _____          Name _____

Address _____          Address _____

_____          _____

Phone _____          Phone _____

Remarks _____          Remarks _____

_____          _____


Name _____          Name _____

Address _____          Address _____

_____          _____

Phone _____          Phone _____

Remarks _____          Remarks _____

_____          _____


Name _____          Name _____

Address _____          Address _____

_____          _____

Phone _____          Phone _____

Remarks _____          Remarks _____

_____          _____

# Pet Shops

Name _____

Address _____

_____

Phone _____

Remarks _____

_____

Name _____

Address _____

_____

Phone _____

Remarks _____

_____

Name _____

Address _____

_____

Phone _____

Remarks _____

_____

Name _____

Address _____

_____

Phone _____

Remarks _____

_____

# Pet Grooming

Name _____

Address _____

_____

Phone _____

Remarks _____

_____

Name _____

Address _____

_____

Phone _____

Remarks _____

_____

Home is where the food is.

# Pet Food

Name _____          Name _____

Address _____          Address _____

_____          _____

Phone _____          Phone _____

Remarks _____          Remarks _____

_____          _____

Favorite brands _____

_____

_____

_____

_____

_____

_____

# Kennels

Name _____          Name _____

Address _____          Address _____

_____          _____

Phone _____          Phone _____

Remarks _____          Remarks _____

_____          _____

## Pet Transport

Name _____     Name _____

Address _____     Address _____

_____     _____

Phone _____     Phone _____

Remarks _____     Remarks _____

_____     _____

## Nearby Police and Fire Stations

Name _____     Name _____

Address _____     Address _____

_____     _____

Phone _____     Phone _____

Remarks _____     Remarks _____

_____     _____

**Previous Owners** _____

_____

_____

**Identification ("lost cat" information)** _____

_____

_____

# Word gets around

Has your cat's name ever found its way into print? If so, keep the article. Some day you may want to show it to your cat. Once a swelled head, always a swelled head.

# FAMOUS LAST WORDS (yours, not your cat's)

**STEPHEN BAKER** is an advertising executive (he created "Let Your Fingers Do the Walking" campaign), an award-winning designer and art director, columnist, and author of 21 books, including three on cats. His own cat inspired this one. He lives in New York City.

**GERRY GERSTEN** is a renowned humorous illustrator whose work has appeared in just about every major publication. He too has firsthand experience with the feline species. He (and his cats) make their home in Weston, Connecticut.